Think on These Things

Shaping Your Destiny Through the Transformation of
Your Thought Life

Michael A. Carter

sermontobook
.com

Unless otherwise specified, all Scripture quotations are taken from the New King James Version®. Copyright © 1982 by Thomas Nelson, Inc. Used by permission. All rights reserved.

Scripture quotations marked (AMP) are taken from the Amplified® Bible (AMP). Copyright © 2015 by The Lockman Foundation. Used by permission. www.Lockman.org.
Scripture quotations marked (CEV) are taken from the Contemporary English Version. Copyright © 1991, 1992, 1995 by American Bible Society. Used by Permission.
Scripture quotations marked (GNT) are taken from the Good News Translation® (Today's English Version, Second Edition). Copyright © 1992 American Bible Society. Used by permission.
Scripture quotations marked (KJV) are taken from the King James Bible. Accessed on Bible Gateway. www.BibleGateway.com.
Scripture quotations marked (NASB) are taken from the New American Standard Bible® (NASB), copyright © 1960, 1962, 1963, 1968, 1971, 1972, 1973, 1975, 1977, 1995 by The Lockman Foundation. Used by permission. www.Lockman.org.
Scripture quotations marked (NIV) ® are taken from the Holy Bible, New International Version ®. Copyright © 1973, 1978, 1984, 2011 by Biblica, Inc.® Used by permission. All rights reserved worldwide.

Scripture quotations marked (TLB) are taken from The Living Bible copyright © 1971 by Tyndale House Foundation. Used by permission of Tyndale House Publishers Inc., Carol Stream, Illinois 60188. All rights reserved.

Sermon To Book
www.sermontobook.com

Think on These Things / Michael Carter
ISBN-13: 978-1-945793-73-8
ISBN-10: 1-945793-73-2

To my beautiful wife, who is my champion and my heartbeat. You have encouraged me from the very beginning to put legs to my dreams, and I certainly wouldn't be the person I am without you.

To my wonderful children, who have treated me with more respect, love, and affection than I deserve. We've had some high notes and a few low notes, but we always make beautiful music.

To my church family, The Life Church. Your support has been more than I've ever imagined. Your love has been inspiring and transforming. "God is not unjust; he will not forget your work and the love you have shown him as you have helped his people and continue to help them" (Hebrews 6:10 NIV).

To Pastora Abigail and Emerlito, to Pastors Tavio and Christie, to Pastors Mike and Val, and to my whole Filipino family. My love for you grows every time I think of you. God has placed us together for His purpose, and I can't imagine life without you. *Mahal kita ng buong puso.*

Praise for *Think on These Things* by Michael Carter

I truly enjoyed and was blessed by reading this book. It was a fun read and so practical for helping the Christian grow more in the Lord. The helpful tips and biblical insights the author provides in this remarkable book will help people think godly thoughts, which lead to a victorious and happy life. ... I would encourage you to purchase this book for equipping church people. It is a delight to use.

Tavio and Christie Raneses
Senior Pastors, The Life Church Davao Oriental, Philippines

Pastor Mike draws the reader's mind to understand the power of choosing the right thoughts over the wrong. He points us to the Savior and [to] the power we have over our thoughts and provides tools that, when employed, change the way we think of ourselves. This is a book that sets God's children apart and sets them on a foundation to success. A must-read for every believer.

Pastor Hudson Bodikwa
Tickyline Faith Center Church, South Africa

If you are a person who enjoys doing a Bible verse study, then this book is for you. *Think on These Things* is a word-by-word study of Philippians 4:8. You will discover that a life governed by the mind of Christ is powerful and life-changing.

Mike and Val Boado
Directors of NEOS Fellowship Center, Tagum City, Philippines

Pastor Mike ably [presents] a scriptural basis for bringing our thoughts into captivity and [managing] how we should think every day. This would be a great Bible study and discussion tool for individuals and groups alike.
Roxy Iverson

Our thoughts form the basis for, and are largely revealed in, our actions and words, and our thought life composes a major part of who we really are. In his book *Think on These Things*, Pastor Michael Carter [has] emphasized the importance of managing our thoughts. [He reminds us] that the Christian's thought life should be focused on the great truths of scripture found in Philippians 4:8. It is with great honor and privilege that I highly recommend this book.
Abigail Penalba
Senior Pastor, JCR The Life Church, Philippines

"As a young pastor, and a lifelong follower of Jesus, my eyes were opened afresh to what the Bible says about the importance of our thought life. Pastor Mike dives into the deep end and shows us how God desires us to think and how to have His thoughts in everything we do. Whether you are new to the Christian life or a lifelong Christian, this practical book will challenge and encourage you in new ways."
Adam Robinson, Staff Pastor, Mannahouse

CONTENTS

Choose Your Thoughts

Everything we are and everything we do begins with a thought.

Most of the time, we do not have a choice concerning the thoughts that come to us. They enter our brains so quickly that there is no stopping them. However, we certainly have the ability to choose what we ponder, the things on which we decide to meditate.

Many people take their thought lives for granted. They think nothing of dwelling on a bad thought or entertaining a dark fantasy. The problem with this is that thoughts are powerful. They lay the foundation for the future, and too often, we don't see the damage until it's too late.

On our honeymoon in Cozumel, my new wife and I decided to take a short cruise and enjoy the Caribbean. During the cruise, we were standing at the back of the boat, looking over into the water. I noticed how much the boat's rudder disturbed the water below, and suddenly, a thought came to me. I didn't ask for this thought; I didn't do anything to bring on this thought. It just came.

The thought was: "If I were to bump into my wife and she fell into the water, no one would ever notice! No one would even know that she was gone. People would ask, 'Hey, what happened to Detra?' I'd say, 'I don't know. She was standing here a minute ago!'"

What a ridiculous thought, right? We hadn't even been married long enough for us to want to push each other into the water. I am joking, of course, but the aforementioned thought did come to me at that moment. I immediately dismissed it, probably because the same thought might have come to her mind! I've come to realize that while we cannot always control the thoughts that come to mind, we certainly have a say in what we do with those thoughts.

It has been said that you are not your thoughts—and that is true. It is important to remember that a thought itself is harmless unless it conceives sin within us. In other words, if we believe the thought and act on it, it will then become a part of us. A thought is simply an object of our awareness. We are not our thoughts, but we are what we think! A thought can be fleeting, but what we think stays with us for a while.

However, you have the power to challenge every thought that enters your mind. You can decide if you want to pay attention to that thought, if you want to change the thought, or if you will ignore it. You can decide whether or not you want to make that thought real. Therefore, when negative thoughts enter your mind and begin affecting your attitude and emotions, simply talk back to them!

Talking back to your thoughts can have a very powerful effect on your life, not only spiritually but practically as well. For example, you can take the thought "I always mess up" and instead choose to think, "When I focus on just doing my best, things tend to turn out well." You choose! You control your thoughts. Imagine the difference you could make in your own life and the positive influence you could have on others if you were to shift your thoughts like this.

God's Word consistently demonstrates the power of our thoughts, but now the latest science also has revealed that thoughts are very powerful, even able to impact us physically. Can you imagine how dangerous it is to entertain negative thoughts if they can impact us in our physical bodies?

Brain imaging clearly shows that when our minds are burdened with many negative thoughts, we tend to become irritable, moody, or even depressed. In his book *Change Your Brain, Change Your Life*, Daniel G. Amen points out that "every thought sends electrical signals throughout your brain. Yes, they have substance, actual physical properties, and they can impact every cell in our body, making us feel either good or bad."[1] Have you ever noticed how you feel physically when you are mentally stressed out?

Daniel Amen goes on to say that even though our thoughts are real, they are often wrong. Our thoughts can lie. If thoughts often support our mental models and our mental models can be wrong—meaning that they are unproductive and no longer serving us well—then some of our thoughts can also be wrong. The lies we sometimes tell ourselves are causing us emotional and physical harm. Therefore, we must change our thinking!

Philippians 4:8 illuminates a powerful strategy for our thoughts:

> *Finally, brethren, whatever things are true, whatever things are noble, whatever things are just, whatever things are pure, whatever things are lovely, whatever things are of good report, if there is any virtue and if there is anything praiseworthy—meditate on these things.*

In this book, I will share with you how to analyze your thought life. I will lay out a plan to capture those thoughts that you tend to dwell on at length, and I will share how to gain control of them. At the end of each chapter, I have provided workbook sections that will help you to refine your thought life. These thoughts will shape the rest of your life. The sooner you can follow the path in Philippians 4:8, the better.

Bill Lewis wrote a fascinating article, "Everything Begins with Your Thoughts." In it, he quotes the following saying: "From the neck down we are all worth minimum wage and from the neck up we have a multimillion-dollar business. Which one do you feed the most?"[2]

He goes on to say, "The sad part is not only are we feeding the minimum wage part more, but we don't protect what goes into the multimillion-dollar part. If we had a 458 Italia Ferrari, we would do everything we could to protect it."[3]

Many of us disregard this principle when it comes to our minds and our ways of thinking. We let almost anything go into our brains without considering the ramifications. Everything we interact with in this life is communicating something to us. We generally don't filter what messages we allow into our brains. A lot of the messages we are hearing take us further away from God and the success He brings. We need to learn to control our thoughts and stay sharp at all times.

Focusing on the positive gives us strength and faith. Focusing on the negative gives us a sense of loss and depression. The positive builds up; the negative tears down. The positive brings boldness; the negative brings fear. The positive brings freedom; the negative brings bondage and, eventually, destruction.

Fortunately, God has given us control over fear and bondage by setting a choice in front of us—the choice to control our thoughts. I'm going to help you get there.

This is the beginning of a new future and destiny. It will positively affect your attitude, your actions, and even how you feel on a day-to-day basis. Your whole body will be impacted once you gain control of your mind and focus on the goodness God has for you.

As you begin your way through this book, read it slowly. Take the time to consider how your own thoughts line up with God's perfect will for those thoughts. Then get ready to make some tough but very important changes.

CHAPTER ONE

The Power of Your Thought Life

I feel an incredible attachment to my spouse and my kids. After all, I chose to get married, I willingly said those vows, and I chose to have kids. I am responsible for these relationships, and at the same time, I would feel helpless without them.

You may know exactly what I'm talking about, or perhaps you're deeply attached to something besides family, such as a job or a hobby. We all have things in our lives that we feel we couldn't live without, and they greatly impact us every single day of our lives.

However, there is something that has even greater control over us than these attachments: our thoughts.

It's easy to think that your mind is off limits to God. After all, how harmful can some thoughts be? It's not like you're ever going to act on them, right? The Bible teaches something different.

Second Corinthians 10:5 tells us that we are to bring every thought under the obedience of Christ. Why would God want this if our thoughts are harmless?

A Harvard research study focused on how thoughts affect the structure of the brain. The study involved two groups of people who had never played the piano before. One group played scales every day, while the second group thought about playing the scales but didn't physically do it. The results showed that the part of the brain that corresponds with finger movements (from piano playing) had grown considerably in both groups. So, even though half of the people in the study had only thought about playing the piano, they had still changed their brains—just as if they had been physically playing the scales.[4]

Our thoughts are hugely powerful, and this study shows that to the brain, thoughts and reality are the same!

Unseen Danger

Have you ever taken the time to consider the impact that your thoughts have on your life? Too many people simply accept life as it comes to them. They assume that things are the way they are and they'll never change. They assume this because they don't realize that their thought life is the foundation of their circumstances and their destiny. When you keep your thoughts focused on negativity, anger, resentment, or even apathy, that's what you'll get.

When you focus on the things of God, you will begin to see God's Word manifest in your life in a tangible way.

Your entire life will then shift in the direction of obedience to God.

In his book *The 4:8 Principle*, Tommy Newberry writes that "mental discipline is the ability to keep your thoughts consistently focused."[5] Our problem isn't limited to what we choose to dwell on. Our problem can also be that we don't dwell on the right things long enough. We let our minds wander from topic to topic. When that happens, we don't get anywhere. Even if every thought is good, we will not grow and move forward if we allow our minds to stay unfocused and chaotic.

People often pride themselves on the ability to multitask. While it's great in a pinch, multitasking has a serious downside. David Rock, the cofounder of the NeuroLeadership Institute and the author of the book *Your Brain at Work*, says, "[Multitasking] reduces our intelligence, literally dropping our IQ.... We make mistakes, miss subtle cues, fly off the handle when we shouldn't, or spell things wrong."[6]

If these are the outer manifestations of multitasking, think about what's happening in our brains when our thoughts are essentially multitasking, jumping from one thing to the next. I can only imagine the unseen mess that we create in our own minds.

To make matters worse, distraction feels great. "Your brain's reward circuit lights up when you multitask," Rock says, meaning that you get an emotional high when you're doing a lot of different things at once.[7]

So, we become addicted to chaos. We become focus-averse. We become hooked on the very thing that is actually holding us back.

Instead, we need to be intentional about what we are doing and what we are thinking. We need control over our thoughts and our focus. Here is a better formula to follow:

Watch your thoughts; they become words.

Watch your words; they become actions.

Watch your actions; they become habits.

Watch your habits; they become your character.

Watch your character; it becomes your destiny.[8]

Understanding the Carnal Mind

Why is it so important to control our thoughts? Aren't some of us logical and some of us emotional, and doesn't God use both kinds of people because He needs our different skills and talents? Wouldn't it be wrong to try to be someone we're not or someone who is the same as everyone else?

The fact is that both the logical/thinking personality and the emotional/creative personality can be carnal. Both sides can lead you away from the Kingdom of God, for it's not our words or actions that determine our goodness, but the thoughts and motives behind them.

Only God knows our thoughts, and He shares this concept with us in His Word:

Because the carnal mind is enmity against God; for it is not subject to the law of God, nor indeed can be.

—Romans 8:7

Then the LORD saw that the wickedness of man was great
in the earth, and that every intent of the thoughts of his
heart was only evil continually.

—Genesis 6:5

Reforming the carnal mind is not part of God's plan for the life of any Christian. Instead, He wants us to put on the mind of Christ. God wants His children to have His thoughts and His priorities. Our thoughts establish our true identity and make us who we really are. Proverbs 23:7 states, "For as he thinks in his heart, so is he."

Ever since the fall of man in Eden, man's carnal mind has driven him further from God until God ultimately destroyed the world because of the evil thoughts and imaginations of the carnal mind. If we are to be mature children of God in this world, we must retrain our minds to think like God thinks.

To do this, the Bible tells us to meditate on God's Word (Psalm 1:2), but what does that really mean? It means nothing more than keeping scriptural thoughts, such as grace, God's overcoming power, and His unconditional love for you, in your mind continually and thinking about them throughout the day. When we meditate on these positive, God-centered messages, then that's what we're going to focus on. That's what will take center stage.

When you think carnal thoughts, then you will be carnal. But if you think overcoming thoughts, you will overcome.

Furthermore, Joshua 1:8 tells us that meditating on God's Word is the formula for a life of prosperity and "good success." When God speaks of success and the abundant life, He is speaking of our total being, including our relationships, our finances, peace for ourselves and being peacemakers for others, our authority in this world, strength to overcome, discernment, foreknowledge, wisdom, and everything else we need in our lives here on earth and in the life to come.

With this understanding in place of what it is to meditate and what can result, we can now dig even deeper to discover how to meditate in a godly way.

The Mind Is a Battleground

Meditating on God's Word is how we must retrain our minds.

There is a war taking place within our minds due to the thoughts, both good and bad, that constantly come into our minds. These thoughts span our past experiences—things we have done or might have done and what others have done to us—as well as what we may do in the future.

The controlled, trained mind knows that when life treats you cruelly or unfairly, it doesn't work to meditate on the cruelty or unfairness you have experienced. Instead, the God-focused mind meditates on God's Word, as David did. In Psalm 119:78, David shared his strategy for dealing with unjust circumstances: "Let the proud be ashamed, for they treated me wrongfully with falsehood; but I will meditate on Your precepts."

Yes, all kinds of thoughts come into our minds, but we choose the ones on which we will meditate. We choose the negative or the positive. The overcomer will put on and keep on the mind of Christ. He or she will choose to meditate only on the thoughts of the Father. The one given over to the carnal mind will dwell on destructive thoughts that lead to even more grief, hurt, anger, and sin.

If you don't understand the importance of being an overcomer, the war that is being waged against your mind will see to it that you receive a constant barrage of thoughts that direct you away from the Father.

> *For we wrestle not against flesh and blood, but against principalities, against powers, against the rulers of the darkness of this world, against spiritual wickedness in high places.*
> **—Ephesians 6:12** *(KJV)*

These wicked spirits, principalities, and powers are constantly trying to rule over you and control you, but they can control you only if they control your mind. That's where the war is fought.

Our Enemies

We have established that there is a war going on right now, at this very moment, over your thoughts. In this war for your thoughts, you face two different types of enemies: outward enemies and inward enemies.

Outward enemies appear to us as other people. However, we are not to wrestle with other people; we are to love them. That's why we are to bless them when they curse us, be good to them when they hate us, and pray for them when they use us and persecute us (Matthew 5:44).

Inward enemies are those thoughts within us that cry out for vengeance and satisfaction, that seek to get even. These are our real enemies! We must wrestle against, overcome, and destroy all of those selfish urges within us. The true overcomers, the mature children of God, will defeat their inward enemies while they continue to love their outward enemies.

Just as our most dangerous enemies are within us, so are the means to defeat them:

> *For the weapons of our warfare are not carnal but mighty in God for pulling down strongholds, casting down arguments and every high thing that exalts itself against the knowledge of God, bringing every thought into captivity to the obedience of Christ....*
> **—2 Corinthians 10:4–5**

We don't need physical weapons to win the battle for our minds; we need the wisdom and discipline to take control of our thoughts. We need to take hold of every thought that comes into our minds and make it obedient to Christ.

The Mind of Christ

We are called to have the "mind of Christ" (1 Corinthians 2:16), but first we need to define what having the mind of Christ actually means. Having the mind of Christ is what happens when God's thoughts become our thoughts. The mind of Christ should override our own selfish, fleshly urges and desires, causing our thought life to be renewed.

Let each of you look out not only for his own interests, but also for the interests of others. Let this mind be in you which was also in Christ Jesus....
—Philippians 2:4–5

And do not be conformed to this world, but be transformed by the renewing of your mind, that you may prove what is that good and acceptable and perfect will of God.
—Romans 12:2

We cannot manifest Jesus to this world if we are thinking with any mindset other than the mind of Christ. Retraining our thoughts and the way we think will transform us into the image of Jesus Christ (Romans 8:29). This requires a complete renovation of our minds.

This is not a passive process. It takes work, and it isn't always comfortable. We have to be humble enough to admit the wrong things we have done, open enough to change our ways of thinking, and diligent enough to pay attention to our thoughts.

Once we are able to overcome the old way of thinking, we will begin to experience the abundant life that Jesus came to give us. This moves us beyond anything our carnal minds could accomplish and allows us to develop the seed of God's Word and make it manifest in our lives.

Jesus alluded to this in the parable of the sower (Matthew 13:1–9, 18–23). Some seed brought forth thirty-fold, some sixty-fold, and some a hundredfold—but it all started as the exact same seed! The only difference was the soil. If the soil was bad, then the seed couldn't grow. If it was good, then the seed produced fruit.

According to the National Institute of Food and Agriculture (NIFA), soil not only supports plant growth and affects water and air quality, but also affects agriculture productivity and sustainability.[9] If we look at our minds as soil, we can see that the mind is a dynamic resource that supports our growth, productivity, and sustainability. We need to pay attention to the seed we're planting, and we also need to make sure that the soil we're planting the seed in is fertile.

If our minds are carnal, the Word of God cannot live for very long. However, when we cultivate the soil where the seed is planted, our minds and hearts, God's Word becomes productive and brings about change both within us and through us.

The Danger of Temptation

God designed us to have a certain kind of creative power. We have the ability to turn our thoughts into incredibly detailed images. We also have the ability to take our thoughts and produce results. Negative, angry, bitter, resentful thoughts will produce results in keeping with those thoughts. Pure, loving, beautiful thoughts will produce that type of result.

Every thought we cultivate, nourish, and water in our minds will grow and bring forth fruit, either good fruit or evil fruit. God created our imaginations to be tools, and we can use them for good or for evil.

We are not subject to our thoughts, but rather, our thoughts are subject to us. Your mind is like a supercomputer, and as powerful as that supercomputer is, it will only do what you program it to do. That's why it is possible for us to bring "every thought into captivity to the obedience of Christ" (2 Corinthians 10:5).

Whether a thought is conceived in our spirit or it is a fiery dart from the outside, it cannot actually turn into anything unless we focus on it. When we keep our focus on Christ, then only the good thoughts from God's plans will bear fruit in our lives. The carnal things, whether they are truly evil or simply human musings, will die away.

What happens if they don't die away? What happens when we are early in this transformation process and we still haven't quite gotten the hang of always focusing on Christ?

Ezekiel 8:12 in the King James Version refers to "the chambers of his imagery." The New King James Version uses the phrase "the room of his idols." Thoughts are images, and the mind is a chamber of imagery. The Lord sees every image and thought upon which we allow our minds to dwell.

You may never have committed the physical act of adultery, but Jesus said that if you are lusting in your mind, you are already guilty of the very act (Matthew 5:28). You may never have committed a murder, yet the Bible says you're guilty of murder if you hate your brother (1 John 3:15).

God is holding us accountable for our thoughts because He understands the power of the mind. Improper thoughts should always be rejected. A thought that you reject, no

matter how wicked it is, is not sin! Lust that is not conceived in the mind is not sin. James 1:15 tells us, "Then,
when desire has conceived, it gives birth to sin; and sin,
when it is full-grown, brings forth death."

When a sinful thought enters your mind, you must
make the decision not to "conceive" it. Many people feel
condemned simply because they have bad thoughts, but
these thoughts, in and of themselves, are merely tempta-
tions, not sin. Jesus was tempted, but He never let a sinful
thought be conceived in His mind by dwelling or meditating on it.

> Blessed is the man who endures temptation; for when he
> has been approved, he will receive the crown of life which
> the Lord has promised to those who love Him.
> —*James 1:12*

When a negative thought comes to you, it may be
tempting for you to dwell on it, but you will overcome the
thought if you reject it. That thought may return, but you
can reject it each time. Keeping bad thoughts out of your
mind so they do not conceive sin is called enduring temp-
tation.

Controlling Your Thought Life

> O Jerusalem, wash your heart from wickedness, that you
> may be saved. How long shall your evil thoughts lodge
> within you?
> —*Jeremiah 4:14*

Many people struggle in life in one way or another, and most believe that they are victims of circumstance. They honestly believe that they have no control over the seemingly inescapable events in their lives. But that is untrue. Our thought life has a profound effect on what manifests in our daily lives.

What you think about is what you will ultimately bring about. We may not be able to control an initial thought, but we can control what we do with it. We have control over what we allow our minds to dwell on, and we are responsible for entertaining positive, biblical thoughts.

> No lions are ever caught in mouse traps. To catch lions, you must think in terms of lions, not in terms of mice. Your mind is always creating traps of one kind or another and what you catch depends on the thinking you do. It is your thinking that attracts you to what you receive.[10]
> **—Thomas Dreier, industrial editor**

What Thomas Dreier says here is very biblical. It tells us that, rather than reacting to the world around us, when we think about or meditate on something, we will attract it. It also says that we will receive the things on which we meditate. If we focus on our own powerlessness, then we will get what comes at us. On the other hand, if we focus on what God says about us and we seek to take charge of the circumstances around us, then we will be empowered and proactive.

Facts may be facts, but all things, even facts, are subject to the Word of God. The Lord gives us creative power, and He also gives us authority. That is why God tells us where to focus our thoughts:

> *Finally, brethren, whatever things are true, whatever things are noble, whatever things are just, whatever things are pure, whatever things are lovely, whatever things are of good report, if there is any virtue and if there is anything praiseworthy—meditate on these things.*
> **—Philippians 4:8**

This verse will serve as the foundation for the rest of the book as we break down the kinds of thoughts that will put us in the right position to live a God-focused life.

Your thought life is very important to God because it governs every single facet of your life. That's why we need to live out our lives filled with God's thoughts. Just think about a life governed by the mind of Christ! Imagine the power in that!

We must control our thoughts because they are the catalysts for our actions and, ultimately, the state of our hearts. Our thoughts govern everything else that we will ever do with God. If we spend our days meditating on His Word, holding every fact we encounter up against the facts of the Bible, then we will have the mind of Christ. This will give us faith and confidence to live out everything God puts in our hearts.

That is my hope and prayer for you, for me, for everyone who comes alongside Christ and desires to be like Him.

WORKBOOK

Chapter One Questions

Question: What does it mean to meditate on God's Word? What are the blessings of doing so?

_____

_____

_____

_____

_____

_____

_____

_____

_____

_____

_____

Question: What does it mean to have the mind of Christ? How can a believer think like Jesus?

_____

_____

_____

_____

_____

_____

_____

_____

_____

_____

Question: What role does your imagination play in your thought life? Is it a help or a hindrance?

_____

_____

_____

_____

_____

_____

_____

_____

_____

_____

_____

_____

Action: Discipline yourself to pay attention to what you are thinking. For a whole day, keep a running list of your thought topics. These are things you spend time dwelling on, not every random thought that enters and immediately exits your mind. It may be helpful to set a timer and then update your list every thirty minutes. At the end of the day, review your list. Which thoughts are God-centered, and which are self-centered?

Chapter One Notes

CHAPTER TWO

Whatever Is True

You cannot have a positive life and a negative mind.[11]
—Joyce Meyer

If we are supposed to meditate on things that please God, we need to understand what those things are. What kinds of things reflect the mind of Christ? We're going to tackle that question throughout this book, and we'll start by discussing the importance of meditating on truth.

In the previous chapter, we learned about our thoughts, the fleeting ideas that come into our minds all day and all night long. We must take control of them, holding on to the ones that reflect God's thoughts while rejecting all others. We must also pay attention to what we meditate on. We need to be intentional about the thoughts on which we focus and concentrate.

The first test to determine the worth of any thought is the test of truth.

Truth Seeker

The Bible tells us to think on what is "true" (Philippians 4:8), but what does that mean?

Merriam-Webster defines *true* as "being in accordance with the actual state of affairs; conformable to an essential reality; fully realized or fulfilled."[12]

This definition is not very far off from the meaning of the word *aletheia*, which is the word for *true* found in the original text of Philippians. *Aletheia* means "trustworthy, fixed, and genuine."[13]

We can safely say that when Paul told us to think about "whatever things are true" (Philippians 4:8), he meant for us to think about things that are true! We are to think about things that are real and genuine, rooted in reality and actuality.

To put it in perspective, the opposite of something true would be a deception, a lie, or a false reality, whether of your own creation or someone else's. I think of false religions, false teachings, and false gods. Gossip, hearsay, and fabricated stories come to mind when I think about the opposite of truth. Each one of those is to be avoided at all costs.

> For those who live according to the flesh set their minds on the things of the flesh, but those who live according to the Spirit, the things of the Spirit. For to be carnally minded is death, but to be spiritually minded is life and peace. Because the carnal mind is enmity against God; for it is not subject to the law of God, nor indeed can be.
> —**Romans 8:5–7**

The relationship between truth and holiness is similar to that between light and vision. Light cannot create an eye or give a blind person his vision, but it is essential to seeing. Wherever light penetrates, it dissipates darkness and brings everything into view.

In a similar manner, truth cannot regenerate or impart spiritual life, but it is essential to the practice of holiness. Wherever truth penetrates, it dissipates error and reveals everything for what it really is, rather than what is manifest or assumed.

Even more than that, Jesus is truth. In John 14:6, Jesus said, "I am the way, the truth, and the life. No one comes to the Father except through Me."

Truth is not simply made up of facts; it is far more than facts. Truth is not just something we act upon. Truth acts upon us. We can't change the truth, but the truth can change us. It sanctifies us, setting us apart from the misrepresentations woven into our sin natures.

Just as Jesus, who is the living Word (John 1:14), is truth, so His written Word is equally truth. Though "heaven and earth will pass away," God's truth will never end (Matthew 24:35).

Truth is reality. It's the way things really are. What seems to be and what really is are not always the same. To know the truth is to see things accurately. To believe what isn't true is to be blind. Truth is true, whether we believe it or not.

The Danger of Not Thinking on Truth

While some people think that to be untruthful is to make up malicious lies, it really is more subtle than that.

When we speculate, we think about things that are not true. Because we don't have all of the information, our brains try to fill in the gaps with whatever we think might fit. When we do that, we create lies that we may go on to believe as truth.

Here's an example: Your child is out past curfew. You begin to speculate as to what could possibly be going on, and your brain takes you down a path of picturing your child drinking or using drugs or running with the wrong crowd. In reality, your child may have a perfectly reasonable explanation for his or her tardiness. But instead of waiting for truth, you choose untruth when you speculate on the situation.

Other forms of untruth are gossip and false witness. These are dangerous, damaging, and sinful. They are rooted in untruth.

We must resist the pragmatism of our culture, which measures truth by whatever fits the situation. In this mindset, we think that if something brings us happiness or accomplishes what we want, then it must be true. However, God's Word doesn't always line up with what works for us and makes us happy. We must test everything by the Word of God, not by our own feelings or the results it might achieve.

First Thessalonians 5:21 says, "Put everything to the test. Accept what is good" (CEV). Additionally, James 1:17 says, "But whatever is good and perfect comes to us from God" (TLB). If it doesn't come from God, then it isn't good!

Those things that society and culture say you must accept, those negative things that a parent or teacher has said about you, and even those things you have come to believe about yourself because of past failures don't measure up when juxtaposed with God's Word. Yet, we often continue to believe those things because they seem reasonable.

For example, maybe you've consistently been a C student, and someone told you that some people are just C students and you should accept the fact that you are one. However, the Bible says that even in tribulation and peril, "we are more than conquerors" (Romans 8:35–37).

We can believe what God's Word says about us because it is true. In the first verse of the Gospel of John, we read, "In the beginning was the Word, and the Word was with God, and the Word was God" (John 1:1). John continued, "And the Word became flesh and dwelt among us" (John 1:14). This is referring to the Word of God being manifest as Jesus, the Man.

Remember that Jesus said, "I am the way, the truth, and the life" (John 14:6). He is not a type of truth or one of many truths, but *the* truth. In other words, He is the only truth. There is no other truth but Jesus; therefore, there is no other truth but God's Word.

He Offers Help

One of the most helpful things I have learned about the Christian life is that all sin begins in our thoughts, which the Bible often calls "the heart." Therefore, if we want to grow in godliness, we must win the battle over sin on the thought level.

Galatians 3:13–14 shows us how:

> *Christ has redeemed us from the curse of the law, having become a curse for us (for it is written, "Cursed is everyone who hangs on a tree"), that the blessing of Abraham might come upon the Gentiles in Christ Jesus, that we might receive the promise of the Spirit through faith.*

If you have never really taken the time to think about your thought life, the idea of capturing every single thought can feel overwhelming. The facts may make this sound daunting, but there is truth to these words. The truth is that you have been redeemed from the curse, so you are not trying to fight this battle on your own.

Being redeemed means many things, including the following:

1. You have freedom from the curse of the law (Romans 8:2).

2. You have been bought with a price (1 Corinthians 6:20).

3. Christ has made you free (Galatians 5:1).

4. You are forgiven (1 John 1:9; Psalm 103:3).

5. Your diseases are healed (1 Peter 2:24; Psalm 103:3).

6. You have peace (Psalm 119:165; Isaiah 57:19;
   John 14:27; Philippians 4:7).

The truth also says that God has good works prepared
for you:

For we are His workmanship, created in Christ Jesus for
good works, which God prepared beforehand that we
should walk in them.
                                        —Ephesians 2:10

God, who desires to lead us by His Spirit, would like
to lead us to the place in our lives where we serve Him.
God will lead us to exactly the right spouse, church, edu-
cation, job, and calling when we set our thoughts on Him
and look to find His truth in our daily lives.

In the Bible, Abram, later renamed Abraham, was led
by God to the place prepared for him, which led to blessings in his life and in his family and lineage for
generations.

Now the LORD had said to Abram: "Get out of your country,
from your family and from your father's house, to a land
that I will show you. I will make you a great nation; I will
bless you and make your name great; and you shall be a
blessing. I will bless those who bless you, and I will curse
him who curses you; and in you all the families of the earth
shall be blessed."
                                        —Genesis 12:1–3

Abraham was called "a great nation" and "a blessing." I don't know what you've been called. Maybe people called you names that hurt you, or maybe someone spoke something over your life that set you on a specific course, for good or for bad. But I'm here to tell you that God calls you great. More than that, He calls you a blessing!

The blessing of God is not a single event; it encompasses an entire life (John 10:10). God will "supply all your need according to His riches in glory by Christ Jesus" (Philippians 4:19). He will exceed your greatest expectations (Ephesians 3:20). The blessing was on Abraham, and others benefited from it. The same is true in your life when you carry the promise of the Spirit through your faith.

Being filled with the Spirit of God allows you to speak and understand mysteries and to walk in authority in every situation. It leads you in all truth and teaches you how to live according to the Kingdom of God.

Winston Churchill said, "The truth is incontrovertible. Malice may attack it, ignorance may deride it, but in the end, there it is."[14]

God's Word is truth. God is truth. Hebrews 11:6 says that "he who comes to God must believe that He is." As you meditate on God's Word, you will see your life begin to transform into a manifestation of His miraculous truth.

Chapter Two Questions

Question: What does it mean to think on what is true? What is the difference between facts and truth?

_____

_____

_____

_____

_____

_____

_____

_____

_____

_____

_____

Question: How is speculation a sin against the truth? What do you think about the idea that all sin begins in our thoughts? Have you experienced this in your own life?

_____

_____

_____

_____

_____

_____

_____

_____

_____

_____

Question: The blessing of God is not an event; it is a life. What are the inherent blessings that come with redemption? How does thinking on truth for your life change the facts of your life?

_____

_____

_____

_____

_____

_____

_____

_____

_____

_____

_____

_____

Action: We may not be able to control an initial thought, but we can control what we do with it. We also have control over what we put into our minds. Look closely at the music, media, and other voices you are putting or allowing into your mind. Are these voices speaking life-giving truth or destructive lies? Choose a day to write down the message behind every voice in your life—friends, co-workers, songs, movies, and so on. Evaluate their messages based on the truth of God's Word.

Chapter Two Notes

_____

_____

_____

_____

_____

_____

_____

_____

_____

_____

_____

_____

_____

_____

_____

_____

_____

_____

_____

_____

_____

_____

CHAPTER THREE

Whatever Is Noble

For I say, through the grace given to me, to everyone who is among you, not to think of himself more highly than he ought to think, but to think soberly....

—Romans 12:3

There is a classic Christmas story by O. Henry entitled "The Gift of the Magi," from his book of short stories *The Four Million*.[15] In this story, Christmas is around the corner, but a husband and wife are very poor. The wife decides to go out of her way to get her husband a surprise gift. She cuts her beautiful hair so that she has enough money to buy him a chain for the pocket watch he cherishes. When he returns from work, he's shocked at her new haircut. He reveals that he sold his pocket watch to buy her some beautiful combs!

It's a touching story that shows what it means to set aside your own desires, wishes, and pride so you can lift someone else up. I find it to be a great example of the biblical definition of being noble.

Something to Strive For

What do you think of when you hear the word *noble*? You may think of haughtiness, arrogance, or prestigious status. However, the meaning of the word *noble* in Philippians 4:8 is much different from that. In a scriptural sense, being noble involves being humble and putting the needs of others above your own.

Being noble means that you put the well-being and happiness of others ahead of your own well-being and happiness. It means that your success positively affects others around you. It means being honest and brave in a way that others admire. A noble action is one that you do for the sole purpose of helping other people.

Nobility speaks to our character, just as truth does. When we choose to speak, act, and live in a spirit of nobility, we make a huge statement to the world around us. But, of course, choosing the noble path does not come easily at first.

The Challenge of Nobility

If this is what it means to be noble, then how does nobility affect our thought life? What does it mean to think on "whatever things are noble" (Philippians 4:8)? Let's look at Paul's assessment of the Bereans in Acts:

> *These were more noble than those in Thessalonica, in that they received the word with all readiness of mind, and*

searched the scriptures daily, whether those things were
so.

—Acts 17:11 *(KJV)*

The people at Berea did three things that Paul called "noble." They received the Word, they readied their minds, and they searched the Scriptures daily. Paul was saying that these people were developing character. They were meditating on Scripture and looking for ways to use it in their daily lives. Their minds were set on God and His Word, and they strongly desired to put the insights they gained to use in their homes, communities, and personal lives.

The Word of God is powerful truth. It cleans you, it guides you, and it dares you to live a noble life. For example, in Matthew 5:44, Jesus said, "Love your enemies, bless those who curse you, do good to those who hate you, and pray for those who spitefully use you and persecute you."

Who wants to pray for their enemies? Who would ever want to do good to their enemies? I can think of a number of times I've wished bad things upon my enemies, and here God is telling me that I need to do only good.

This is the challenge of being noble. Not many people, in the natural way of being and doing things, would be excited by those instructions in Matthew 5. However, chronically failing to obey Jesus can lead to a hardened heart that cannot hear God. Dwelling on hatred and ill wishes for others is a mental state that is difficult to change. Once those thoughts are there, they tend to set up camp and stick around.

Enemies No More

Transforming your mind will require you to transform the way you treat others, even your worst enemies. This is not an overnight thing, but something that will develop from within you. The more you take the path of the Bereans and receive the Word, ready your mind, and search the Scriptures daily, the more you will find that it changes who you are. Your desires will change, the way you see others will change, and your actions will change. You will begin to put others first, even those who once may have been your worst enemies.

Be open to hearing the Word and acting on it. Acts 17:11 says that the people "received the word with all readiness of mind" (KJV). They could not wait to hear the Word of God. They had an expectation. They expected the blessing of the Lord. This encouraged and strengthened them, and it will do the same for you today.

> But those who wait for the LORD [who expect, look for, and hope in Him] will gain new strength and renew their power....
> —*Isaiah 40:31 (AMP)*

When you hope in God, studying His Word, praying to Him, and trusting Him, you will not be disappointed. As 2 Timothy says, "Study and do your best to present yourself to God approved, a workman [tested by trial] who has no reason to be ashamed, accurately handling and skill-fully teaching the word of truth" (2 Timothy 2:15 AMP). This is your first step toward a noble mind.

Do Something Nice

While we are definitely in a battle against immoral forces today, where we are is actually nothing new. There have always been, in one form or another, hatred, racism, slavery, murder, strife, lying, cheating, stealing, prostitu-tion, mind-altering abuse, and an attack on the Word of God.

In other words, scriptural nobility has always struggled to flourish. When it has flourished, like with Mother The-resa, it grabs headlines and gets people talking. So, while it is true that the proverbial gutter is real, it is equally true that it is neither the only reality nor the highest reality.

Life is ennobled when we think on things that are above, and a noble mindset is part of that. Set your thoughts on how you can help others, how you can serve them, and how you can bring glimpses of Jesus into eve-ryday life. As you focus on those things, you create a better world, and you take huge strides toward a purified mind and heart.

WORKBOOK

Chapter Three Questions

Question: What are some characteristics of a noble person? What kinds of thoughts, then, are noble thoughts?

_____

_____

_____

_____

_____

_____

_____

_____

_____

_____

_____

Question: What made the Bereans noble? Are you receptive to God's Word in your life? How does God's Word give someone hope?

_____

_____

_____

_____

_____

_____

_____

_____

_____

_____

_____

Question: How can someone in dismal circumstances be lifted up through thinking noble thoughts? Give an example from the Bible, history, or your own life.

_____

_____

_____

_____

_____

_____

_____

_____

_____

_____

_____

_____

Action: Being noble comes from the act of meditating on our behaviors. Look at your choices, small and big, over the past twenty-four hours. Which ones were noble—that is, sacrificial and thinking of others—and which were self-centered?

Chapter Three Notes

_____

_____

_____

_____

_____

_____

_____

_____

_____

_____

_____

_____

_____

_____

_____

_____

_____

_____

_____

_____

_____

_____

CHAPTER FOUR

Whatever Is Just

Have you ever done something simply because it was the right thing to do?

I think of a story in the news not too long ago in which a teenager found a wallet that had $1,500 cash inside. He could have pocketed it and gone on his way. After all, he didn't steal it; he found it. Instead, the teen returned the wallet to the address on the ID.[16]

The news heralded him as a hero. He had done the right thing, even though there was nothing stopping him from simply walking away, money in hand.

That teenager did what was just.

Just and Right

Just in this sense can be defined as "conforming to a standard of correctness" or "acting or being in conformity with what is morally upright or good."[17] The term *just* is taken from the Greek word *dikaios* (DIK-ay-ous), which means "righteous" or "approved by God."[18]

The definition of *dikaios* is "upright, righteous, virtuous, keeping the commands of God, innocent, faultless, guiltless, used of him whose way of thinking, feeling, and acting is wholly conformed to the will of God, and who therefore needs no rectification in the heart or life (i.e., Jesus)."[19]

In a nutshell, *justice* means doing the right, moral thing according to the standards set forth in the Bible. Justice is following the ways of God. A similar term for it is *righteousness*. Living in a way that is just is referred to as living in a "right state."

A right state, for which God and His Word are the standard, is a state in which no fault or defect can be charged. It involves living in such a way that if someone were to speak badly of you, no one would believe it. It means conformity to God's revealed will as well as the act of God establishing a man as righteous.

The Path of Justice

It's important to realize that only God determines what is just. He sets the moral standard for all living things. Psalm 145:17 tells us, "The LORD is righteous in all His ways...." In contrast, Romans 3:10 says, "There is none righteous, no, not one."

On our own, we are incapable of always finding the just path. We may have been taught a few truths of justice when we were growing up. After all, many people, like that teenager who returned the wallet, choose the just path when presented with a dilemma. However, we must understand that it is God who defines that just path in the first place. It is only through His guidance that we can be sure to choose the just path every time and in every circumstance.

The Lord is gracious and just in all He does. When something is just, it conforms to the standard of God. Our human concept of justice is so limited and fallible that we will fail ourselves and each other morally unless we purposefully meditate on God's justice.

It can be easy to think of a court of law when we think of justice, but the form of justice we need to pursue isn't about passing judgment on another person. That is more of a human brand of justice. Instead, God's justice is about becoming like Him and seeing ourselves as He sees us. There are many benefits to looking at justice with this definition. Here are a few:

Justice brings us peace. When we take comfort in being just, it releases the stress of expectations and trying to be good enough, and it releases us from trying to become righteous through our own efforts and actions.

It helps us to have a right perspective. God sees us through the eyes of a crucified and resurrected Christ, with forgiveness of sin and the power of the Holy Spirit on our side. Therefore, we can stop dwelling on our failure and focus on overcoming it and maintaining God's righteousness in our lives.

It allows us to accomplish God's purpose in our lives. It's difficult for us to move forward in fear. We sometimes hesitate because we don't feel as though we deserve to be or to do what God is prompting us to be or to do. But when you live justly, you can rest in God and move forward in your purpose!

Join God's Justice League

In Philippians 4:8, Paul wrote, "Whatsoever things are just ... think on these things" (KJV).

God is the source of all just things, and the only way for us to be in tune with His justice is to be in tune with Him. We can strive to live a just life all we want, but we will fail if we aren't focusing on Christ. As we meditate on the truth that God is justice and He imparts His justice to us, we will see transformation of our minds and our actions.

We can have peace and purpose in our lives when we meditate on God's justice. Start by focusing on what it means to be just as God defines justice. Then magnify it throughout your life!

Chapter Four Questions

Question: What is a biblical definition of *just*? How does it move beyond the human concept of *fair*?

_____

_____

_____

_____

_____

_____

_____

_____

_____

_____

Question: What are some of the benefits of justice—that is, conformity to the standard of God? Which benefit encourages you the most? Why?

_____

_____

_____

_____

_____

_____

_____

_____

_____

_____

Question: What are examples of thoughts that are rooted in a clear understanding of God's justice? What is the relationship between God's justice and social justice? What sort of actions will come out of thinking on that which is just?

_____

_____

_____

_____

_____

_____

_____

_____

_____

_____

_____

_____

Action: Write a list of things, from the silly to the serious, that make you angry. Beside each one, write out an appropriate "just thought" that gives God's perspective on that issue.

_____

_____

_____

_____

_____

_____

_____

_____

_____

_____

_____

Chapter Four Notes

_____

_____

_____

_____

_____

_____

_____

_____

_____

_____

_____

_____

_____

_____

_____

_____

_____

_____

_____

_____

_____

_____

_____

CHAPTER FIVE

Whatever Is Pure

It happens when we least expect it, sometimes in our dreams. We're going about our day, and an unsettling thought suddenly flashes into our minds. It can be from a television show or movie we watched. It can come from a book we read or a conversation we had. Usually, the thought is sexual or violent or tainted in some way. It is impure.

It's true that we have little control over the flitting images and ideas that flash through our minds, so how do we take control of these dirty, unsettling thoughts? How can we focus on that which is pure?

A Pure Mind

Pure can be defined as "unmixed with any other matter; free from dust, dirt, or taint."[20] This definition means that something pure has nothing added to it.

A pure thought about sex would be free of lust and perversion, and it would be with your spouse. A pure thought about a frustrating situation would be free of anger, violence, and malice. It would view the situation from a pure stance of truly wanting what's best for all parties and understanding that life is intricate and people are delicate. But how do we achieve pure thinking when we are so consumed by our sin nature?

Pure comes from the Greek word *hagnos* (HAG-nahs), which means "innocent; holy; without defect."[21] If we are going to think on pure things, it follows that they have to come from a pure source. Any thought not coming from a pure source will be tainted and damaged, full of defects.

The only original source that exists in the universe is God, and the reason we know this is because He is the only one who was there in the beginning.

> In the beginning was the Word, and the Word was with God, and the Word was God. He was in the beginning with God.
>
> —*John 1:1–2*

But how can we think on only godly things when everyday life is full of human sin? Does this mean we need to throw out our televisions, unplug our Internet, and downgrade to dumb phones?

While we'd probably benefit from doing all of those things, there's something to keep in mind: God doesn't tell us to get saved and then become righteous or pure. He doesn't leave us on our own to figure things out, just waiting for us to mess up our lives. No, God saves us, and then

He makes us righteous. This means that right now, at this very moment, you have the ability to know what things are pure and think on those things.

Fighting Impurities

God is the original source, and God is pure, but there are things that can contaminate God's purity in our lives. These things mix with His Word and contaminate the image we have of ourselves. We need to catch ourselves when we are mixing in impurities. We need to take those things back to God's Word and see what He says about us and our situation. Remember, truth is truer than fact.

There are six common things that can contaminate our self-image: envy, anger, strife, worry, negative words, and negative thoughts. When these things pollute our thoughts, they can limit God's ability to work in our lives. God wants to work through us to make an example to the world and to those over whom we have influence. Therefore, concentrate on what God says about you. You are His dwelling place!

> *Or do you not know that your body is the temple of the Holy Spirit who is in you, whom you have from God, and you are not your own?*
> **—1 Corinthians 6:19**

This all comes back to the thoughts we think and the focus we have in our lives. When certain thoughts come against our minds, we can maintain pure thoughts and lives by focusing on the good things of God, rather than the situations swirling around us.

Furthermore, the Bible says that we speak "out of the abundance of the heart" (Luke 6:45). Therefore, if we focus our hearts and minds on what is pure, we don't have to be as concerned about what we say. Our words are a reflection of our thoughts, so if our thoughts are pure, our words will be pure.

> *Let no corrupt word proceed out of your mouth, but what is good for necessary edification, that it may impart grace to the hearers.*
>
> **—Ephesians 4:29**

> *Not what goes into the mouth defiles a man; but what comes out of the mouth, this defiles a man.*
>
> **—Matthew 15:11**

In Matthew 15:11, Jesus was talking about Jewish customs, but He was also making a point to us today. We can be defiled by what comes out of our mouths. This means that what we allow to occupy our thoughts and swirl around in our minds will eventually come out, and we will be blessed or defiled by it.

Getting control over the things we put into our minds, pushing away unclean thoughts, and focusing on God's Word will profoundly impact our lives. However, we cannot do this alone. God created us, and He alone knows us thoroughly. He cleansed us with the blood of His Son, Jesus.

David said, "Search me, O God, and know my heart; try me, and know my anxieties; and see if there is any wicked way in me, and lead me in the way everlasting" (Psalm 139:23–24). Opening your heart to God makes way for Him to root out the impurities hiding within you so you can grow toward a pure mind and, from that, a pure life.

Live in Purity

From the time we are born, we're inundated with impure thoughts, images, and things in our environment. It takes a near-Herculean effort to remove those things that are not like God so we can be pure. Still, we can do it! We need to focus on manifesting purity in our hearts, our language, and our behavior.

What is it in your life that is keeping you from a more intimate relationship with God? Is it a feeling or an attitude? Is it pride or an erroneous desire? Is there something within you that is displeasing to God?

Remember, it all begins with a thought. If you struggle with meditating on pure things, if you allow the enemy to have sway in your mind, make the decision to take control of your thought life!

Peace of mind, right standing with God, and blessings to yourself and, through you, to others will be your reward if you continually put forth the effort to push away thoughts that are not pleasing to God.

Chapter Five Questions

Question: What are things that contaminate God's purity or image in us? Which of these is the greatest struggle for you?

_____

_____

_____

_____

_____

_____

_____

_____

_____

_____

Question: How can a believer maintain pure thoughts in the midst of a culture saturated with impurity?

_____

_____

_____

_____

_____

_____

_____

_____

_____

_____

_____

Question: What is the connection between your thoughts and your words? How might your words toward others be improved if you were to think on pure things?

_____

_____

_____

_____

_____

_____

_____

_____

_____

_____

_____

_____

Action: Read Psalm 139:23–24 and 1 John 1:9. Spend time asking God to search you and to purify your thoughts of anything that does not please Him.

Chapter Five Notes

_____

_____

_____

_____

_____

_____

_____

_____

_____

_____

_____

_____

_____

_____

_____

_____

_____

_____

_____

_____

_____

_____

CHAPTER SIX

Whatever Is Lovely

Top-selling author and speaker Dr. Robert A. Rohm once said that "someone who constantly thinks about money will generally have better financial results than someone who never gives money a second thought." He went on to say that those who think about friends and family will have more fulfilling, loving, and strong relationships and that those who focus on spiritual things will have more "peace and contentment in their heart." His point was that our thoughts are incredibly powerful in our lives. What we dwell on inwardly will become more of a reality outwardly.[22]

So, what happens when someone thinks on that which is lovely? The definition of *lovely* found in Philippians 4:8 comes from the Greek word *prosphiles* (pros-fee-LACE), which means "acceptable, pleasing." The concept of loveliness is woven throughout the Scriptures, and we see it in Psalms.[23]

How lovely are Your dwelling places, O LORD of hosts!
—Psalm 84:1 (NASB)

Lovely is one of the more interesting words in Philippians 4:8. After all, who doesn't want to think about things that bring joy and delight?

To think about lovely things is to think about that which is pleasant and pleasing to our souls. These are things that make us smile, things that lift us up, things that bring happiness.

How can we know what's lovely? Just as with pure, noble, just, and true thoughts, we have the ability to spot that which is lovely when we are striving to stay close to Christ. When something isn't lovely, it is up to us to identify it and expel it.

Beauty for Ashes

There are people who live their lives circling around whatever grabs their attention. Generally, these are negative things that draw them in with sensationalism and ugliness. An example of this might be what my friends call being "attracted to drama." This applies to situations in which another person experiences trouble, and we find ourselves attracted to the trouble itself, wanting to regurgitate it to others.

Finding pleasure in discord and conflict, whether it is via a reality TV show, a relationship at work, or a news story, is deeply problematic, even if it is done somewhat unintentionally. Some people drawn to ugliness are good people who are pulled in without ever realizing it.

Other people are more intentional in their pursuit of ugliness. Nothing seems to satisfy them more than things that are sinful and immoral. You can tell by the conversations in which they engage, the TV programs they choose to watch, and the books and magazines they read. The consumption of all of these things leads to a vulture-like attitude inside of them.

All of us are capable of falling into this trap of avoiding what is lovely, and how loathsome and repulsive that must be to God. However, instead of discarding us, He chose to think on that which was lovely. He chose to see beauty, and He chose to find joy in His creation, despite our fallen state. His act on the cross changed us from loathsome creatures to things of loveliness.

We still have our sin nature, but there is a path for us to move away from that and toward His perfect, lovely plan. He also took away our sorrow and mourning and, in exchange, gave us a crown of beauty and loveliness.

> To console those who mourn in Zion, to give them beauty for ashes, the oil of joy for mourning, the garment of praise for the spirit of heaviness; that they may be called trees of righteousness, the planting of the LORD, that He may be glorified.
> **—Isaiah 61:3**

So, what is loveliness? It isn't sensuality or sexiness. The word *lovely* can be defined as "attractive or beautiful, especially in a graceful way."[24] Outward beauty can be lovely, but inward beauty that derives from the Holy Spirit is always lovely.

Loveliness can be time spent with a child, teaching him or her about God. It can be a heart that is repentant and turned toward the Creator. It can be a beautiful day, a quiet time in the morning, or a walk along the beach that gives us opportunity to marvel at God's majesty. True loveliness is all around us, and it is always innocent.

If our thoughts are not in line with what is lovely, it's usually easy to tell because we:

- feel bad physically and become more susceptible to ailments
- feel angry or irritated for no apparent reason
- feel depressed
- change directions often
- agree with negative conversations
- feel unsettled and pressured by the things of this world

In addition to weakening your body and mind, not thinking on lovely things has negative social results:

- People won't want to be around you.
- You won't want to be around other people.
- The exceptional will elude you, and you will remain ordinary.

This is why God calls us to think on things that are lovely.

Reaching Toward Loveliness

The first step to living this life is to expose and expel any negative thoughts by intentionally focusing our thoughts on lovely things.

The world-famous Mayo Clinic encourages its patients to practice positive thinking. According to their research, the results of positive thinking can include: "Increased life span, lower rates of depression, lower levels of distress, greater resistance to the common cold, better psychological and physical well-being, better cardiovascular health and reduced risk of death from cardiovascular disease, and better coping skills during hardships and times of stress."[25]

But where do we start? What thoughts will help us?

First, we need to think on things that are lovely about God. Paul wrote, "Now hope does not disappoint, because the love of God has been poured out in our hearts by the Holy Spirit who was given to us" (Romans 5:5).

In *The Living Bible*, this verse reads, "Then, when that happens, we are able to hold our heads high no matter what happens and know that all is well, for we know how dearly God loves us, and we feel this warm love everywhere within us because God has given us the Holy Spirit to fill our hearts with his love" (Romans 5:5 TLB).

Think about how great and vast and wide God's love for you really is. Consider how you do not deserve His love, yet He still forgave you and provided a way for you to live an abundant, fulfilled, successful life.

Secondly, think on things that are lovely about yourself. David wrote, "I praise you because I am fearfully and wonderfully made; your works are wonderful, I know that full well" (Psalm 139:14 NIV).

You are a complex being made by God, and you have great value. "You were bought at a price" (1 Corinthians 6:20), and "the very hairs of your head are all numbered" (Matthew 10:30).

It doesn't matter what you've done or what you've been through. If you give God your heart, He will take care of the rest. All of the charges against you have been dropped, and all of the evidence that condemns you has been destroyed. You are justified.

We also need to think on things that are lovely about others. Ephesians 4:2–3 instructs us on how to have a positive attitude toward other people: "Be humble and gentle. Be patient with each other, making allowance for each other's faults because of your love. Try always to be led along together by the Holy Spirit and so be at peace with one another" (TLB).

When another person gets the feeling that you don't really see much good in him or her, that person is less likely to take the time to see much that's good in you. Seeing the good in others is a simple but very powerful way to feel happier and more confident and to live a more loving, peaceful, and productive life.

Lastly, we need to think on things that are lovely about life. We will magnify whatever we focus on. When we think about the blessings in our lives, they become even more real to us. Even in the worst circumstances, we can find something in our lives that is worth celebrating.

What in your life brings you joy? What in your life brings joy to others? What are your dreams for your future? By focusing on these lovely things about your life, you will help them to grow.

Lovely Benefits

A life of lovely thoughts is a life filled with joy and positivity. After all, it's nearly impossible for negativity and sadness to creep in when the opposite things are already so dominant!

The more you think upon that which is lovely, the more you'll notice that people will want to be around you and you will want to be around them so you can share your joy. You'll notice that you are healthier and more energetic. You'll find that exceptional things will come your way as God blesses your positive, joyous outlook.

Will there be struggles? Sure. Job was a man of joy in God, yet he was challenged immensely (Job 1:1). However, in the end, he was also immensely blessed (Job 42:12–16). God loves to love a joyful spirit. He loves the lovely.

Start today by letting go of grudges, flouting envy— and instead, be appreciative, kind, and gentle. Rejoice in the Lord a little more each day. Take pleasure in beauty and virtue. Clear away the cobwebs of doubt, frustration, and anger from your life. Let your mind dwell on Christ, and He will beautify your situation.

This is incredibly important, "For we are His workmanship, created in Christ Jesus for good works, which God prepared beforehand that we should walk in them"

(Ephesians 2:10). God desires us to be close to Him and to reflect His thoughts and His leading, and an essential part of that is a lovely outlook.

WORKBOOK

Chapter Six Questions

Question: What is a person's condition apart from God? How has He made you lovely?

_____

_____

_____

_____

_____

_____

_____

_____

_____

_____

_____

Question: What tempts you toward thoughts of ugliness
or sadness? What are some of the benefits of thinking on
that which is lovely?

_____

_____

_____

_____

_____

_____

_____

_____

_____

_____

Question: Do you think lovely thoughts toward yourself?
Toward others? What are some specific negative thought
patterns you have, and how can you replace them?

_____

_____

_____

_____

_____

_____

_____

_____

_____

_____

_____

_____

Action: Find or make a beautiful print of a favorite verse or quote that will encourage you to think on that which is lovely.

Chapter Six Notes

_____

_____

_____

_____

_____

_____

_____

_____

_____

_____

_____

_____

_____

_____

_____

_____

_____

_____

_____

CHAPTER SEVEN

Whatever Is Virtuous

By now we've firmly established the effect your thought life has on your attitude, your actions, and your destiny. Your thought life can also affect the quality of your everyday life and, in some cases, the length of your life. There is one more thought focus we need to tackle, and that is virtue.

What do you think of when you hear the word *virtue*? Does it conjure ideas of Victorian-era public morality or some system of archaic rules that must be followed? Really, virtue, as it's used in our key scripture for this book, has more to do with character than behavior.

Virtue can be defined as "a conformity to a standard of right, moral excellence; a beneficial quality or power of a thing."[26] It comes from the Greek word *arete* (ah-reh-TAY), which means "excellence of character."[27] Other versions of our key verse use the word *excellent* in place of *virtue*. Some synonyms for *excellent* are "superb, outstanding, exceptional, and magnificent."[28]

Scriptural virtue is about character. A virtuous person is exercising each of the previously discussed characteristics: truth, nobility, justice, purity, and loveliness. A virtuous person has these attributes so locked in that they have changed his or her character. People of virtue are always excellent in their interactions with others, with their words, in their attitudes, and in their compassion.

According to 2 Peter 1:5–9, God doesn't add virtue to our character; it is our responsibility:

> But also for this very reason, giving all diligence, add to your faith virtue, to virtue knowledge, to knowledge self-control, to self-control perseverance, to perseverance godliness, to godliness brotherly kindness, and to brotherly kindness love. For if these things are yours and abound, you will be neither barren nor unfruitful in the knowledge of our Lord Jesus Christ. For he who lacks these things is shortsighted, even to blindness, and has forgotten that he was cleansed from his old sins.

Notice that virtue leads the charge. It is the first thing we are to strive for, and the others will follow. How does this work if virtue is the result of character and character is the result of our thoughts? Does this mean that we first must change our thoughts, then our character, and then we can work on perfecting our faith? That seems like a tall order, but this is where God comes in. He knows the right recipe for your life.

A Virtuous Command

God doesn't have to get your feedback when giving you instructions for your life. He already knows what you need. He laid out several reasons for virtue, and then He told us to add virtue to our character. Because God is omniscient (all-knowing, all-wise, and all-seeing) and because God lives in eternity, He has already been there and seen the results. That's why He can confidently tell you what you need to do to bring the best outcome.

Even though God already knows what we need, He still gives us a choice along with His command. That shows how much He loves us. He wants to be in a willing relationship with us. He gives us the tools to have a great life, but He doesn't force them on us.

Second Peter 1 gives us five reasons for adding virtue to our character. These show that God has given you what you need to thrive. There is no excuse for living a worrisome, frustrated, compromising, godless life when God has so clearly provided this help.

First, God has given us everything we need for a successful, thriving life: "His divine power has given to us all things that pertain to life and godliness" (2 Peter 1:3a). Second, God has "called us by glory and virtue" (2 Peter 1:3b).

Third, God gives us an identity that is unmistakable. He has given us incontrovertible, incontestable, unquestionable, and unchangeable promises. Our promises to each other can sometimes be broken, and they only mean as much as we can offer. In other words, our promises are limited because we are limited. God is unlimited; therefore, His promises are sure. Not only are they sure, but they are also "exceedingly great and precious" (2 Peter 1:4).

Fourth, He made us "partakers of the divine nature" (2 Peter 1:4). When God calls us to become part of His family, we actually partake in His divine nature. We are eternal beings with the very nature of God.

Fifth, He saved us from corruption (2 Peter 1:4). We have the ability to live above our circumstances. We are able to live our lives above corruption, dishonesty, offense, and immorality.

Peace That Surpasses Understanding

One of the most impactful results of virtue is that it brings peace.

The thing about worry is that it is, for the most part, self-inflicted. One of the ways that we inflict worry on ourselves is by living unethical and dishonest lives. When we strive to live virtuous lives, God brings peace to us. He takes all of our concerns and cares and lifts the burden of worry from our shoulders, and we realize that He truly is in control.

The following verses demonstrate that, and they also lay out some of the qualities of virtue:

> *So the church throughout Judea and Galilee and Samaria enjoyed peace [without persecution], being built up [in wisdom, virtue, and faith]; and walking in the fear of the Lord and in the comfort and encouragement of the Holy Spirit, it continued to grow [in numbers].*
>
> —*Acts 9:31 (AMP)*

YOU HAVE LOVED RIGHTEOUSNESS [integrity, virtue, upright-ness in purpose] AND HAVE HATED LAWLESSNESS [injustice, sin]. THEREFORE GOD, YOUR GOD, HAS ANOINTED YOU WITH THE OIL OF GLADNESS ABOVE YOUR COMPANIONS.
—Hebrews 1:9 *(AMP)*

Therefore, believers, be all the more diligent to make cer-tain about His calling and choosing you [be sure that your behavior reflects and confirms your relationship with God]; for by doing these things [actively developing these virtues], you will never stumble [in your spiritual growth and will live a life that leads others away from sin]....
—2 Peter 1:10 *(AMP)*

Virtue hates lawlessness; it walks in fear of the Lord and in the comfort of the Holy Spirit. It goes hand in hand with peace, wisdom, and faith. It is godliness, brotherly kindness, and love.

Show me someone who does a good job, and I will show you someone who is better than most and worthy of the company of kings.
—Proverbs 22:29 *(GNT)*

Excellence isn't some unreachable, lofty goal that we cannot achieve. God expects excellence out of us because He is excellent. Since we have His DNA, we have the ca-pacity to be excellent as well—at everything!

If we take God at His Word, which we well should do, and we add these virtues to our lives, we will never fail, not in a heavenly sense. A virtuous life is also a victorious life.

The Company of Kings

When we cleanse our minds and adopt God's way of thinking, our character changes. When our character changes, we begin to experience what it is to live in virtue. Only then can our faith and relationship with God truly come into full view.

Imagine living without worry or stress or fear, knowing that you have an eternal purpose that is much more compelling than earthly goals. Every one of us should desire to live a satisfying and purposeful life, striving to become whole and complete as we walk our journey. Every one of us should determine to be worthy of the company of kings, and God has provided us with the keys.

Won't you put them into practice? Won't you shed old habits that are getting you nowhere and turn to His righteous way? The life awaiting you is more than you can imagine.

WORKBOOK

Chapter Seven Questions

Question: Whose responsibility is it to add virtue to your life? What are the benefits of doing so?

_____

_____

_____

_____

_____

_____

_____

_____

_____

_____

Question: How does virtue lead to a peaceful life?

_____

_____

_____

_____

_____

_____

_____

_____

_____

_____

_____

Question: How is the idea that a virtuous life is a victorious life in opposition to the message of the world? What does it mean to be victorious in the Christian life, and how is this different from worldly success?

_____

_____

_____

_____

_____

_____

_____

_____

_____

_____

_____

_____

Action: Read and memorize Philippians 4:8. Consider how your thoughts need to change to align with these categories. Then come up with a game plan. Start with the area that needs the most work and decide how you are going to change your thinking to reflect God's will for your mind and your life.

Chapter Seven Notes

_____

_____

_____

_____

_____

_____

_____

_____

_____

_____

_____

_____

_____

_____

_____

_____

_____

_____

CONCLUSION

Change Your Mind

What thoughts dominate our time and our minds? We are often so occupied with the cares of life that we have little recollection of the thoughts and ideas we entertained during the day, yet these thoughts are directly related to the outward chaos that surrounds us!

In fact, it has been medically proven that our thoughts will affect our immune system:

> Dr. Michael Jacobson cited a study in which patients were asked to recall various types of emotional experiences while doctors monitored how it affected their bodies. Each patient was asked to relive the experience in their minds for five minutes.
>
> When the patients thought for five minutes about experiences that made them depressed, they found out that it affected the patients' immune system and their antibody levels dropped 55%. Six hours later, their immune system was still depressed.
>
> But when the patients thought for five minutes about situations that made them happy, their antibody levels rose

40% and it was still elevated six hours later. ("Stress and the Heart" Dr. Michael Jacobson, October 1996). This is medical evidence that the thoughts we think affects [sic] our bodies, either positively or negatively.[29]

What seeds are we unknowingly planting for our future? What kind of harvest are we setting up for ourselves?

Hebrews 11:1 says, "Now faith is the substance of things hoped for, the evidence of things not seen." If you and I don't work to keep our minds focused on the things in which we believe and that we cherish the most, we will certainly reap an unwanted harvest.

We must realize that our thoughts will bring about the strongest results in our lives. Take the time to listen to what is going on in your mind as you drive down the street, as you sit in the waiting room, as you work, as you shop, and as you carry on conversations with others.

God gave us a choice at creation. He gave Adam and Eve a choice between life and death. They chose death by eating of the forbidden tree (Genesis 3:1–13). They listened to the enemy. It was a one-time decision that has forever affected humanity. It was a one-time thought that led to a one-time action that led to eternal consequence.

We still do this today when we choose not to operate in our God-like character. We do this today when we choose to dwell on the types of thoughts that will bring us down. When we make these choices, we are far from the image of God.

Every day, you have the opportunity to pull it together. You have the opportunity to make a new choice—a better choice—and listen to the Word of God rather than the enemy.

It won't be easy. There are times when the enemy will cause you to doubt that you heard God at all. He will plant confusion and skepticism. But you must choose to be strong and persevere, trusting that the promises God set out in His Word will swoop in and save the day.

Bigger Than You Think

The branch of science called epigenetics tells us that the decisions we make today, such as pursuing addictions or wrong eating habits, can become substances in our brains that affect the genetic structure of our bodies. These things can then be transferred genetically to our children.[30]

The serious nature of this becomes clear when we read in Exodus 20:5 that God punishes the children of those who hate Him to the third and fourth generations. The choices you make today have long-term consequences. When you choose negative thoughts, you are choosing not to walk in the way of the Lord. At that point, you have made idols over and above the knowledge of God, and your children are watching.

It's important to know that Jesus took this very seriously. In Matthew 18:6, He said, "If anyone causes one of these little ones—those who believe in me—to stumble, it would be better for them to have a large millstone hung around their neck and to be drowned in the depths of the sea" (NIV).

You must rewire your brain! As Romans 12:2 admonishes us, "do not be conformed to this world, but be transformed by the renewing of your mind, that you may prove what is that good and acceptable and perfect will of God."

You Have the Power

Paul's strategy to rewire his brain is found in 2 Corinthians 10:3–5. His main weapons were his knowledge of Jesus Christ and the power of the Holy Spirit. You have access to this divine power combination as well! You have been given the ability to destroy arguments and every thought raised against or contrary to the knowledge of God. You have what you need to cleanse your mind.

Moreover, you have the ability to take every bad thought captive and make it obedient to Christ and who Christ is. You have everything you need to control every negative thought that comes your way. You just need to think about your thoughts. You need to get into Scripture. You need to meditate on God and open yourself to His transformative power.

Thomas Edison, the great inventor, once said, "Five percent of the people think; ten percent of the people think they think; and the other eighty-five percent would rather die than think."[31]

Why are we afraid to take the time to think, to ponder and contemplate with focus? If you want results, you need to take intentional action. Begin changing your thoughts and your mind today by opening your Bible and taking in the Word. That is the first step, and through that step, the rest will fall into place. Remember this: Toxic thoughts equal a toxic life. Healthy thoughts equal a healthy life.

REFERENCES

Notes

1. Amen, Daniel G. *Change Your Brain, Change Your Life*. Revised and expanded ed. Potter, 2015.

2. Lewis, Bill. "Everything Begins with Your Thoughts." *Life Leadership*. October 9, 2013. http://bill-lewis.net/2013/10/09/everything-begins-with-your-thoughts.

3. Lewis, Bill. "Everything Begins with Your Thoughts."

4. Begley, Sharon. "The Brain: How the Brain Rewires Itself." *TIME Magazine*. January 19, 2007.

5. Newberry, Tommy. *The 4:8 Principle*. Tyndale House, 2007.

6. Rock, David. *Your Brain at Work*. HarperCollins, 2009.

7. Rock, David. *Your Brain at Work*.

8. "Watch Your Thoughts, They Become Words; Watch Your Words, They Become Actions." *QuoteInvestigator.com.* https://quoteinvestigator.com/2013/01/10/watch-your-thoughts. There is conflicting information on the origin of this quote; however, the earliest evidence of this quote is from Frank Outlaw, the creator of a supermarket chain called Bi-Lo.

9. "Soil Programs." *National Institute of Food and Agriculture / United States Department of Agriculture.* https://nifa.usda.gov/program/soil-programs.

10. "Thoughts Sermon Illustrations." *More Illustrations.* http://www.moreillustrations.com/Illustrations/thoughts%202.html.

11. Meyer, Joyce. *Battlefield of the Mind.* FaithWords, 2008.

12. "True." *Merriam-Webster.* https://www.merriam-webster.com/dictionary/true.

13. Strong, James. "G225 – alētheia." *Strong's Exhaustive Concordance of the Bible.* Hunt & Eaton, 1894.

14. Thnay, Vincent. *The ABC of Quotes.* Lulu Press, 2015.

15. Henry, O. "The Gift of the Magi." *The Four Million.* The McClure Co., 1908.

16. "Teen Returns Wallet Filled with $1500 Cash." *CNN.com.* September 20, 2017.

https://www.cnn.com/videos/us/2017/09/20/californi
a-teen-returns-cash-filled-wallet-orig-trnd-lab.cnn.

17. "Just." *Merriam-Webster*. https://www.merriam-webster.com/dictionary/just.

18. Strong, James. "G1342 – dikaios." *Strong's Exhaustive Concordance of the Bible*. Hunt & Eaton, 1894.

19. "Dikaios." *BibleStudyTools.com*. https://www.biblestudytools.com/lexicons/greek/nas/dikaios.html.

20. "Pure." *Merriam-Webster*. https://www.merriam-webster.com/dictionary/pure.

21. Strong, James. "G53 – hagnos." *Strong's Exhaustive Concordance of the Bible*. Hunt & Eaton, 1894.

22. Rohm, Robert. "What You Think About You Bring About." *Personality Insights*. https://www.personality-insights.com/tip-what-you-think-about-and-talk-about-you-bring-about.

23. Strong, James. "G4375 – prosphilēs." *Strong's Exhaustive Concordance of the Bible*. Hunt & Eaton, 1894.

24. "Lovely." *Merriam-Webster*. https://www.merriam-webster.com/dictionary/lovely.

25. "Positive Thinking: Stop Negative Self-Talk to Reduce Stress. *Mayo Clinic*. https://www.mayoclinic.org/healthy-lifestyle/stress-

management/in-depth/positive-thinking/art-20043950.

26. "Virtue." *Merriam-Webster.com*. https://www.merriam-webster.com/dictionary/virtue.

27. Strong, James. "G703 – aretē." *Strong's Exhaustive Concordance of the Bible*. Hunt & Eaton, 1894.

28. "Excellent." *Thesaurus.com*. http://www.thesaurus.com/browse/excellent?s=t.

29. Crockett, Kent. "Thinking: Our Thoughts Affect Our Immune System." *Kent Crockett*. http://www.kentcrockett.com/cgi-bin/illustrations/index.cgi?topic=Thinking.

30. Dias, Brian G., and Kerry J. Ressler. "Parental Olfactory Experience Influences Behavior and Neural Structure in Subsequent Generations." *Nature Neuroscience* 17 (2014), p. 89–96.

31. Kirov, Blago. *Thomas Edison: Quotes and Facts*. 2014.

About the Author

Michael Carter and his wife, Detra, are the senior pastors at The Life Church in Bloomington, Indiana. Pastor Mike is a graduate of Indiana Wesleyan University in Business Science and Religious Studies.

Pastor Mike and his wife pioneered and pastored the Abundant Life Family Worship Center in Indianapolis, Indiana, for three years before returning home to become senior pastors of The Life Church. They served as worship leaders at The Life Church for seven years and as elders for three years.

Pastor Mike has spoken to congregations around the world, including in the Philippines, Romania, and Fiji. He and Detra have five children—four girls and one boy.

About Sermon To Book

SermonToBook.com began with a simple belief: that sermons should be touching lives, *not* collecting dust. That's why we turn sermons into high-quality books that are accessible to people all over the globe.

Turning your sermon series into a book exposes more people to God's Word, better equips you for counseling, accelerates future sermon prep, adds credibility to your ministry, and even helps make ends meet during tight times.

John 21:25 tells us that the world itself couldn't contain the books that would be written about the work of Jesus Christ. Our mission is to try anyway. Because in heaven, there will no longer be a need for sermons or books. Our time is now.

If God so leads you, we'd love to work with you on your sermon or sermon series.

Visit www.sermontobook.com to learn more.